MW00512695

HANDBOOKS OF EUROPEAN NATIONAL DANCES

EDITED BY
VIOLET ALFORD

※※ ※※

DANCES OF FRANCE

II: Provence and Alsace

Plate 1   La Volto.   Provence: *Marseilles costume*

DANCES of FRANCE

II: Provence and Alsace

NICOLETTE TENNEVIN

and

MARIE TEXIER

NOVERRE PRESS

TRANSLATED BY
VIOLET ALFORD
ILLUSTRATED BY
LUCILE ARMSTRONG
ASSISTANT EDITOR
YVONNE MOYSE

First published in 1953
This edition published in 2021 by
The Noverre Press
Southwold House
Isington Road
Binsted
Hampshire
GU34 4PH

ISBN 978-1-914311-15-4

CONTENTS

✳✳✳✳

Illustrations in Colour, pages 2, 12, 29, 39
Maps of Provence and Alsace, page 6

ALSACE

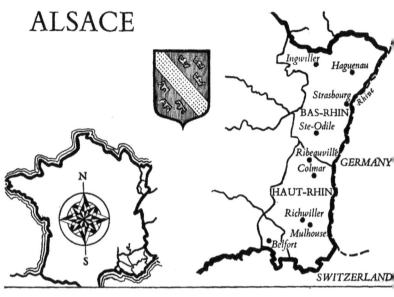

Ingwiller · Haguenau
· Strasbourg
BAS-RHIN
Ste-Odile
Ribeauvillé
· Colmar
HAUT-RHIN
Richwiller
· Mulhouse
Belfort
Rhine
GERMANY
N
S
SWITZERLAND

PROVENCE

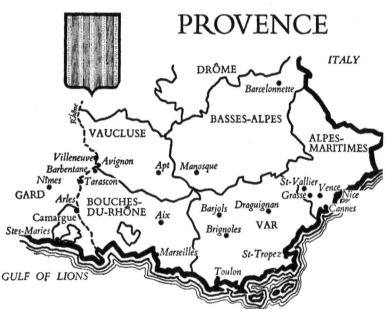

DRÔME
Barcelonnette
ITALY
BASSES-ALPES
VAUCLUSE
ALPES-
MARITIMES
Villeneuve · Avignon
Barbentane
Nîmes · Tarascon
GARD
Arles
Camargue
Stes-Maries
BOUCHES-
DU-RHÔNE
Apt · Manosque
Aix
Barjols · Draguignan
Brignoles
VAR
St-Vallier · Vence
Grasse · Nice
Cannes
Rhône
Marseilles
St-Tropez
GULF OF LIONS
Toulon
MEDITERRANEAN SEA

DANCES OF PROVENCE

BY NICOLETTE TENNEVIN

One of the regions of France richest in traditions is the old province and kingdom of Provence. Direct heiress from ancient Greece and later Rome, her very name points out her classic heritage—Provence, the first Roman province in Gaul. A country flooded with sunshine, vibrating with warmth and the whirring song—if song it can be called— of the cicada, its people have always shown a gay, *insouciant* spirit which manifests itself in song and dance, procession and festival. This gay temperament was developed by the famous Provençal troubadours, especially under Good King René in the fifteenth century, to whom so many and various organisations, customs and songs are imputed. In the early sixteenth century *La Basse Danse* by Arena gives us the names of several dances then in fashion in Avignon and Aix-en-Provence, together with a strange picture of the manners of his day. The Mal Maridada was an old dance even then and is a widespread folk-song theme today. Branles were in fashion, and at Carnival time 'fine Morisques' and the Antigalliagaya, a pair dance with '*pantomime extrêmement obscène*'. Arena was sufficiently musical to concern himself with airs, the well-known Fricassée for instance. He then kindly advises dancing young men not to scratch their heads for lice nor to dribble at the mouth.

Later we get a glimpse of Provençal determination to dance what they prefer—their own Rigaudon, which afterwards was carried to courts and ballrooms and became the rage in Paris and London. Here, in its own home, it was regarded by ecclesiastics as 'an invention of the devil, indecent in all its movements, really scandalous with *pantomimes infâmes*'—words applied to the Antigalliagaya so long

7

before. But the people of Vence undertook a lawsuit against their own Bishop in defence of their favourite dance, which was carried to the regional Parliament and even to the Privy Council of Louis XIV.

This gay dancing spirit came to a second fruition in the eighteenth century, encouraged by the trade corporations which, until the Revolution, organised fêtes in honour of their patron saints. The Church too, in spite of the perpetual struggle between priests and people on the subject, organised great festivals and processions in which ceremonial dances had a large place. The poet Mistral carries the history into the nineteenth century, telling us in *Calendal* of dances practised in his time: La Gavotte, supposed to be the source of the Court Gavotte and thus named from the *Gavots*, the peasants of Haute Provence; La Martegale, and the Brande di Gusas, which earned as bad a name for itself as the Rigaudon, and was still done somewhat secretly in Mistral's day when the country folk had feasted and well drunk. It was perhaps from this Brande or Branle that the Carmagnole sprang, that dreaded revolutionary Chain dance; and both belong to the Farandole family.

✤ A CLASSIFICATION ✤

Provençal dances may be roughly classified in four groups (which, of course, overlap in many cases):

1. Those once belonging to trades, generally Corporation or Guild dances.

2. Real folk dances, performed by the people at any of their fêtes.

3. Dances practised by the old noblesse and high Provençal society.

4. Ritual dances, traditional to country folk and townsmen, performed only on special occasions.

Corporation dances. Li Courdello (the Strings or Ribbons) may have been a trade dance. A pole about 7 ft. high decorated with hanging ribbons is carried to the centre of the dancing-place and there held. Girls and men each take the end of a ribbon and, threading in and out, plait them round the pole, then reverse the movement and un-plait. The step is a springy Polka step, and the dance is what English people persist in calling a Maypole dance. The Courdello pole is not a Maypole, is not planted in the ground and is not confined to the month of May.

Li Tisseran (the Weavers)—again a trade dance. A light framework representing a loom is hung with ribbons; the dancers, after dancing round the frame, take each an end and move up to the frame and back from it again, while a man, the Weaver, with something in his hand to represent the shuttle, weaves another ribbon horizontally in and out of those which hang. La Civaia (the Oats) may once have had a magic intent like the English Oats and Beans and Barley O! It is still a favourite in the high mountain valley of Barcelonnette.

Li Triho (Les Treilles: the Vine Arbour) belongs to vine-yard country only. It shows a promenade under leafy arches, the gathering of the grapes and finally the wine-press. The arches are made of shoots cut from the vines, decorated with their leaves and bunches of grapes. This dance is done by men and women at the grape harvest.

Li Jardiniero (the Gardeners—in the feminine). This is much like the Triho and is done in parts of the country where gardens abound, at Apt, Draguignan and Marseilles. Another occupational dance, Les Bergères, comes down from the Alpine regions with miming in which the men reel the thread off the spindle as shepherds do on the mountains, and the girls spin on an imaginary or real distaff.

The real *Danses Populaires* or folk dances are of great variety, sometimes fusing with those of other categories. Well known is Les Matelotes, performed once by sailors on board their warships at Toulon, and now filtered into sailors' villages, village dancing schools, even into the Farandole itself.

La Fricaissio (La Fricassée: a medley) is a couple dance miming a teasing figure, a sulking figure and of course a reconciliation.

Lou Rigaudoun (Le Rigaudon) has such a varied history that it may be included amongst folk dances proper, especially in Dauphiné round Gap, where most fêtes end with this regional dance; amongst the dances of the noblesse when it went to châteaux and to Court, even amongst ritual dances when used in the great Corpus Christi procession of Aix-en-Provence. Nowadays it is of a round Country-dance type, the girls moving round the ring counter-clockwise, changing partners, thus dancing with each man in turn.

Dances of High Society. Some of these worked through to the people, the Rigaudon for example. This dance travelled to Court and back to its place of origin, where it had been alive all the while.

Another Court dance of an older date is La Volto (the Volta), thought to be of Provençal origin but in reality an Italian importation. Its main feature is the swirling leap performed by the lady, her skirts billowing out like a balloon. The 'Lavolta high', as Shakespeare called it, was much reprobated. Arbeau, the famous author of the *Orchésographie*, tells his pupil to 'dance another dance'; Louis XIII would not allow it at Court. But it got there at last and to England too, living on in Italy all the time.

ꙮ THE FARANDOLE ꙮ

Li Brandi (Les Branles) are simple Rounds, open or closed, related to the Farandole, and so bring us to the Provençal dance *par excellence*, claimed as unique though in reality but one example of the antique Chain dance known from the Black Sea to the Atlantic, from Scandinavia to Greece.*

* See the volumes on *Bulgaria, Greece, Norway, Denmark* in this series.

The Farandole, like the Rigaudon, can be classed differently according to the manner and the moment it is performed—a true folk dance certainly, also a ritual dance or at least a ceremonial one when appearing at Carnival, at weddings or on some grave occasion. La Farandoulo claims descent from the Chain dance of Crete figuring the turns of the Minotaur's Labyrinth; and, considering its Mediterranean affinities together with the proto-historic and classic influences from Greece upon the coast of Provence, there is no reason to reject this antique origin. To-day all sorts of steps are introduced and the antique Chain is held up, faltering in its course, for the men to show off. Competitions for Farandole societies do great harm, inciting innovations and untraditional steps; the best moment to see this noble, antique Chain is after a wedding, or in the Roman arena at Nîmes after a bullfight, when young men, excited by bulls and wine, leap the barricades to form a straining, virile, living chain across the vast circle of sand.

RITUAL DANCES

Provence is still rich in ritual dances, performed chiefly during Carnival and on patronal saints' days. For Carnival we have Li Coco (the Coconuts), by men wearing half-coconuts fixed on knees, elbows, breast and hands. With those on their hands they clap the others and those of other dancers. Their faces are blacked and the ritual Fool attends them. Li Boufet (the Bellows) is a crude Carnival dance with possibly a magical meaning; Li Fieloue (the Spinners) is another, performed by a number of men in white chemises, large collars and flapping hats. With bells on their arms and carrying a distaff lighted by a candle showing through transparent coloured paper they parade at night, improvising satirical verses and dancing.

There are ritual dances accepted by the Church such as those (now vanished) at Manosque, and the Tripettes (from

Plate 2   La Farandoulo.   Arles, Provence

trépigner, to agitate; nothing to do with *tripe* as so often stated) at Barjols, who on St. Marcel's Day jerk about on their chairs or while standing at High Mass.

La Danse de la Souche (Souco) must be some ancient rite—in this land classic origins must not be ignored—taken over by the Church. It was alive before the war at St-Vallier. A Marche de la Souche takes everyone to church; a Prière de la Souche, partly in Provençal, partly in French, is sung to a fine tune. A fire is lit by the priest; the *souche*, a thick old vine-root, is laid upon it, the Farandole is danced round it.

Mauresques were popular on that Saracen-ridden coast, and one of the two Sword dances of France belongs to Provence. The other is the famous Baccubert in a hamlet of Dauphiné pressed against the mountains of the Italian frontier. Les Olivettes is an example of the European hilt-and-point Sword dance but has acquired other elements. It has no special date, appearing at great fêtes and for distinguished guests. Eight to sixteen young men, whose costume has frequently changed, and the Fool, or Harlequin, make up the company. In the middle of Sword-dance figures comes a pole-plaiting figure, the Courdello already mentioned, properly performed by the men, sometimes by intruding girls. A 'lock' of swords is formed round Harlequin, he steps upon it and is raised shoulder-high. A romantic innovation shows girls rescued from the Saracens.

The Chivau Frus, hobby horses, danced in the celebrated Corpus Christi procession at Aix, still appear to the tune Bizet used in *L'Arlésienne*.

ᵐᵍ MUSIC ᵍᵐ

The dance music of Provence has come down through so many generations and has been so modified by musicians, learned and unlearned, that it must be called traditional, not folk music. The songs belong also to this much-worked-on type. We remember the famous Troubadours who re-made songs to the liking of their audiences, and again those newer troubadours, the poets of Mistral's renaissance, who rewrote old songs and composed new ones on ancient Pro-vençal models, so that at last nobody quite knows what is traditional and what is not.

The regional instruments are the pipe and drum played by the same musician but often accompanied by several drummers. These *tambourinaires* are the repositories of tradi-tional airs, often dancing-masters, and are necessary at every village festival. As long ago as Arena, already men-tioned, who wrote in the beginning of the sixteenth century, it was advisable to 'find a tabor-player who knows how to teach properly . . .'. The pipe is of boxwood or ebony with three holes, played with the left hand. The usual pipe is tuned to what is called Saint-Barnabé, in B natural, and measures 10 in.; another, called the Aubagne pipe, is in B flat. They are always played in unison. The 'long drum of Provence' measures 2 ft. 4 in. and is of walnut wood, the two faces covered with calf or dog-skin specially tanned. The top face has a hemp string stretched across diametric-ally, which regulates and limits the vibrations. Other cords on the outside are used for tuning. There is a classic decor-ation running down the length and a long strap by which the drum is hung on the left arm, the left hand holding the pipe, the right hand the drumstick. There has been a revival of these ancient instruments during the last three decades, and *tambourinaires*, although mostly playing by ear, often possess MS. notebooks of tunes which ensure the life of traditional airs for at least another generation.

COSTUME

Every region has its costume, particularly its cap. In the Marseilles region women wore a large black felt hat or a straw one over the lovely lace and muslin cap called *couqueto*. A fitting bodice, cut low, showed the chemise; a fichu, white or flowered, a skirt of quilted patterned cotton called Indienne, an apron, white stockings and flat black shoes completed the costume. The Couqueto was seen not long ago on the Marseilles quays. Men wore knee breeches of cloth or velveteen, gaiters to the knee tied with a red garter. Round the waist is the *taiolo* or sash.

The Arles region boasts a famous dress. It became modified by fashion, and as its general use ceased in the late nineteenth century it bears marks of that date. A long plain dress, a lace fichu pinned into a multitude of little folds in front, a little cap bordered by wide black velvet ribbon on the back of the head, with a stiffened end of the ribbon standing out behind. Men wear white for fêtes, with red or blue sash, small black tie and wide felt hat.

Fishermen on the coast roll their trousers to the knee, wear white, or now brilliant blue, shirts, sash and red stocking cap.

OCCASIONS WHEN DANCING MAY BE SEEN

January 16th, *St-Marcel*	Ancient patronal fête at Barjols. Trépidation at Mass. Procession and killing of ox, dancing round it.
Carnival, especially Shrove Tuesday	Everywhere. Caramentran (a figure) is promenaded, men's ritual dances, disguises. Modern Nice Carnival.
Ash Wednesday	Death and Funeral of Caramentran, dances round the fire.
April 23rd, *St-Georges*	Fête of the Camargue *Gardians* at Arles.
May Day	Fêtes at Nice and suburbs, some remains in villages.

May 17th and near dates	Celebrated Bravade at St-Tropez.
May 22nd	Patronal fête at Draguignan. Hobby Horses and Les Olivettes may perhaps be seen.
May 24th and 25th	Patronal fête at Les Saintes Maries. Gypsies from far countries.
June 23rd, Midsummer Eve	Bonfires everywhere. Dances round the fires. The Tarasque (great dragon) 'runs' at Tarascon.
July 29th, Ste-Marthe	Procession of the Tarasque, now tamed, at Tarascon.
Christmas	The famous Calendal, home and church celebrations, Santon fair at Marseilles, Pastorales and shepherds' masses in some villages.

Provence is rich in fêtes; many are Bravades with much firing of guns. Modern dance groups are often invited to take part in village festivities, and caution is needed by the seeker for true tradition.

SOME GROUPS WHICH PRACTISE THE DANCES OF PROVENCE

La Couqueto, Marseilles.
L'Académie Provençale, Cannes, Avignon and elsewhere.
L'Escola de la Valeia, Barcelonnette, Haute-Provence.
L'Hirondelle, Barbentane, Bouches-du-Rhône.
Lou Riban de Prouvenço, St-Rémy, Bouches-du-Rhône.

And many others.

DANCES OF ALSACE

BY MARIE TEXIER

As in so many parts of France, the nineteenth century saw the disappearance of the real traditional dances of Alsace, a furious fashion for the Polka and the Valse completing their rout. Then came the intrusion of other ballroom dances into the country repertory, and the Mazurka and the Schottische appeared. But here, in Alsace, the Valse still reigns, a Valse in 2/4 time, special to the country and extremely popular. All our dances are sung dances, but can also be performed to the strains of a band. They end all our fêtes, and the youth of the country by no means despises them as so often happens elsewhere.

Our fêtes are numberless, both ecclesiastical—for instance the famous pilgrimage of Ste-Odile—and civil. Some of the latter are historical, dating from the time of Charlemagne and later of Napoleon, and later still to celebrate our double return to our mother-country. All stages of human life are fêtes: baptisms, marriages, the departure of army conscripts; but the most characteristic are those of the land: the cherry harvest in the Lower Rhine country celebrated by a procession under arches decorated with leaves and cherries (this is of modern origin), the gathering of the hops in the Haut-Rhin; the grape harvest, when a men's dance, the Dance of the Winepress, is done at Richwiller; the corn harvest in Haguenau; and the May-time when a girl dressed in white is covered with spring flowers, and made the centre of a round dance by her girl attendants.

A few ancient fairs or kermesses named *Messti* in the Bas-Rhin and *Kilbe* in the Haut-Rhin still exist. The Messti of Oberseebach near Strasbourg is a celebrated local fête in May, where old customs are well observed. There are to be seen decorated wagons and trimmed-up horses all be-ribboned, and processions of young men and girls.

The Bibeltanz, the Cock dance, is still to be seen, one of those affairs beloved of peasants. Here, in Alsace, a tall post is set up with a cross bar at the top. A cock is fastened to one arm of the cross piece; on the other is a lighted candle with a weighted string attached. A Valse begins, the couples spin round below the pole, the string catches fire, burns through and the weight drops to the ground. It is the couple at whose feet the weight falls who get the cock.

⅍ MUSIC ⅍

The Germanic fife was one of the Alsatian instruments also. When brass instruments came into use the excellent brass bands which sound throughout our country came into being, to enliven all our festivities. The violin, the mouth organ and the accordion are not much in favour, finding their sphere in little fêtes and parties only. Our band musicians have a fête of their own, the Pfifferstag (Fifers' Day), which is celebrated with brilliancy at Ribeauvillé and in other places, and dates back to 1390.

The dance airs show interesting affinities with those of Switzerland. The Lauterbach for instance is known in many Alpine regions; the dance itself becomes more de-veloped in the Alps. Dance-songs abound.

⅍ COSTUME ⅍

The costumes of Ingwiller and Mietteschen have spread over the greater part of Alsace, and from regional have become the national costume of the country. They are worn on Sundays, on fête days and at ceremonies.

The women's dress is: a chemisette of fine white linen, gathered at the neck, decorated with lace at wrists and neck; corselet bodice of black velvet or cloth; little coloured silk shawl with fringe. The skirt is full and ankle-length, with two bands of black velvet or brocaded silk ribbon a few inches from the hem. Women of the Roman Catholic Church wear red skirts, women of the Protestant Church green, Jewish women mauve. The apron is of bright brocaded silk falling nearly to the skirt-hem. A ribbon goes round the waist, brought to the front and knotted with long ends, and sometimes a bib covers the corselet. White stockings, black buckled or strapped shoes. A gold cross hangs from a black velvet ribbon round the neck.

The head-dress is one of the most striking in France. On a small round cap which fits the top of the head is fixed the famous butterfly bow of red or black stiff silk ribbon, plain or brocaded, the two ends being fringed. This ribbon is about 8 inches wide. It is simply tied in a huge bow, loops of the same size, and two ends hanging behind.

The men wear trousers of black cloth, the pockets of which are decorated with three gold buttons. The short waist-length coat has revers with one or two rows of small gold buttons; the waistcoat is of bright red cloth, the shirt white with a black tie. White socks and low black shoes. The hat is black felt with a broad brim, or a fur cap.

OCCASIONS WHEN DANCING MAY BE SEEN

May Day	In many villages.
May (dates to be ascertained)	Messti or fairs, especially at Oberseebach, near Strasbourg.
Cherry Harvest	Lower Rhine country.
Hop-picking	Upper Rhine country.
Corn Harvest	Especially at Haguenau.
Grape Harvest	Especially at Richwiller, with Danse du Pressoir (winepress) by men.

THE DANCES

TECHNICAL EDITORS
MURIEL WEBSTER AND KATHLEEN P. TUCK

✳✳✳✳✳✳✳

ABBREVIATIONS
USED IN DESCRIPTION OF STEPS AND DANCES

r—right ⎫ referring to   R—right ⎫ describing turns or
l—left ⎭ hand, foot, etc.   L—left ⎭ ground pattern
C—clockwise   C-C—counter-clockwise

For description of foot positions and explanations of any ballet terms the following books are suggested for reference:

A Primer of Classical Ballet (Cecchetti method). Cyril Beaumont.

First Steps (R.A.D.). Ruth French and Felix Demery.

The Ballet Lover's Pocket Book. Kay Ambrose.

Reference books for description of figures:

The Scottish Country Dance Society's Publications. Many volumes, from Thornhill, Cairnmuir Road, Edinburgh 12.

The English Folk Dance and Song Society's Publications. Cecil Sharp House, 2 Regent's Park Road, London, N.W.1.

The Country Dance Book I–VI. Cecil J. Sharp. Novello & Co., London.

POISE OF THE BODY AND HOLDS

The poise of the body is natural and easy in every dance, that of the men more upright than that of the women. In Li Jardiniero the poise of the women is slightly exaggerated due to the holding of half-hoops over the head.

Chain grasp

As in the Farandole, each dancer grasps the one in front with his r hand and the one behind with his l hand. The first and last man places his free hand on his hip.

Valse grasp

In couples. Men grasp partner with both hands on hips; women, facing partner, place hands on men's shoulders and lean away slightly.

BASIC STEPS

	MUSIC
Polka Step	*Counts*
This resembles a Change-of-step, as there is little or no spring.	
STEPS FOR USE IN THE FARANDOLE:—	
Pointing Step	
Hop on l foot, pointing r foot diagonally forward, knee straight.	1, 2
Hop on l foot, crossing r foot in front of l ankle, knee bent and ankle extended.	3
Hop on l foot, pointing r foot forward.	4, 5, 6 (1 bar of 6/8)
Repeat, springing on to r foot and pointing l foot.	(1 bar of 6/8)
Coupé Step. Travel to R.	
Slide r foot sideways, bending r knee and taking weight.	1, 2, 3

Cut l foot under r, landing on l foot (coupé under).	4, 5, 6
Hop on l foot, with r foot behind l ankle.	1, 2
Hop on l foot, with r foot raised in 2nd position.	3
Spring with feet together in 1st position.	4, 5, 6 (2 bars of 6/8)

N.B.—If repeated, still travel to R.

Polka Spring. Travel to R.

Step sideways on r foot.	1, 2
Close l foot to r.	3
Step sideways on to r foot.	4, 5, 6
Spring on to l foot in front of r foot, with r foot behind l ankle, knee bent and ankle extended.	1, 2
Hop on l foot, stretching r foot sideways in raised 2nd position.	3
Spring feet together in 1st position.	4, 5, 6 (2 bars of 6/8)

N.B.—If repeated, still travel to R.

Heel and Toe Step

Hop on l foot, placing r heel in 2nd position; leg turned out.	1, 2
Hop on l foot, with r toe in 2nd position; knee bent and turned in.	3
Spring feet together in 1st position.	4, 5, 6
Hop on r foot, with l foot extended across r ankle.	1, 2
Hop on r foot, stretching l leg sideways in raised 2nd position.	3
Spring feet together in 1st position.	4, 5, 6 (2 bars of 6/8)

Other steps are described as they occur in the dances.

LA VOLTO (The Turn)

tuturuturuturu

Region	Brignoles, Grasse, Marseilles and along the coast of Provence. Costumes from Marseilles (Plate 1).
Character	Quiet at first, working up to a very lively dance.
Formation	For a single couple or any number of couples. Partners stand facing each other round a circle so that the men have their l and the women their r shoulders to the centre. Men start by moving the r foot forward while the women move the l foot backward, the men with hands on partner's waist and the women with hands on the man's shoulders.

Dance	MUSIC *Bars*
FIGURE I: BALANCÉ	A
Step forward on the r foot (woman back on the l).	1 (beat 1)
Bring the l foot to the r with a small circular movement rising on to the toes.	(beat 2)
Pause in this position. (The movements of this bar are called Balancé forward.)	(beat 3)
Repeat, but men dance Balancé backward and women Balancé forward.	2

23

Repeat movements of bars 1–2.	3–4
Repeat movements of bars 1–4.	5–8

FIGURE II: TOURNÉ

Man steps forward on r, turning to R, while woman steps backward on r foot, each turning so that l shoulders are toward partner.	9
Both cross l foot, man in front, woman behind, to make a half-turn. (Man assemblé, woman renversé turn.)	10
Reverse the steps, man stepping backward and woman forward.	11–12
Repeat movements of bars 9–12.	13–16

FIGURE III: SAUTÉ

B

Couples perform a Balancé together; the man then takes his weight on his l foot and makes a half-turn in order to support his partner while she makes a half-turn in the air. Woman steps forward each time on her r foot to prepare for the leap. During the leap the woman slips her r arm round the man's neck from behind, so that her r hand is on his r shoulder while she keeps her skirt down with her l hand. The man helps his partner into the leap by supporting her on each side above the hips.	17–18
Repeat the movements of bars 17–18 three more times, not necessarily on the same spot.	19–24

LA VOLTO

Arranged by Arnold Foster

25

LA FARANDOULO (*The Farandole*)

ᵗᵗᵗᵗᵗᵗᵗ

Region   Lower Provence. Costume of Arles (Plate 2).

Character   Lively and gay. The leader should be a good mime with a sense of humour and capable of originality as well as having a knowledge of suitable steps.

Formation   For any number of dancers in a chain formation with a leader, who holds the r hand of the second dancer with his l. There need not necessarily be an equal number of men and women, but the last dancer should be a man. The leader and the last dancer have their free hand on their hips. As the Farandole was originally danced up and down the village streets and in the squares, the main interest of the dance lies in the ground patterns that are made and in the steps introduced by the leader.

Dance   For the figures a rhythmical walking step is used, and between the figures the leader can introduce any of the steps given on pp. 21–22, or classic steps, which the other dancers try to copy.

Before starting each figure the leader leads the dancers where he wishes, varying the track as he likes.

FIGURE I: THE SNAIL

The leader makes a large circle, gradually making his way toward the centre by winding up the chain of dancers into a snail-shell. When they are sufficiently coiled he unwinds them by leading No. 2 dancer under his l arm, the

LA FARANDOULO

Arranged by Arnold Foster

others following until all are unwound. The leader then walks the chain about before starting Figure II.

FIGURE II: THE BRIDGES

Nos. 1 and 2 face each other with hands joined to make an arch under which the others will pass. Then Nos. 3 and 4 make an arch so that Nos. 5 and 6 will pass under two arches, and so on. The couples are thus used to make a series of arches. When the last arch is made No. 1 leads under, all gradually join on in single file, and the chain is re-formed.

FIGURE III: THE MAZE

The leader walks the chain into a semicircle, then makes a turn and leads under the arms of the dancers behind him so that a plaited effect is obtained:

N.B.—The music is repeated as often as desired as the figures are not danced to any set number of bars. The time taken will vary with the number of dancers in the chain, and will also depend on the number of steps introduced between the figures.

Plate 3
Li Jardiniero.
Provence:
women from
Villeneuve-lès-Avignon,
man from the Carmague

LI JARDINIERO (*The Gardeners*)

| Region | Apt, Draguignan, Marseilles and horticultural districts. Women's costume is from Ville-neuve-lès-Avignon, man's from the Camargue (Plate 3). |

Region   Apt, Draguignan, Marseilles and horticultural districts. Women's costume is from Ville-neuve-lès-Avignon, man's from the Camargue (Plate 3).

Character   Stately and flowing.

Formation   For eight couples. The women hold a half-hoop of flowers, the men a basket of flowers.

Dance

Except for the first Figure, the step used throughout is a Polka or Change-of-step with little or no spring.

MUSIC

INTRODUCTION

Couples walk to dancing-place and arrange themselves as in Diagram 1, men on the outside, women holding hoops over their own heads (○ = woman, □ = man). The verse of song is sung.

Sung verse first time

Diagram 1

FIGURE I: CROSS-OVER

a All take one Polka step sideways to form   1
one line on either side of the dancing-
place, each woman in front of her partner.
Three changes of feet in 3rd position with   2
springs.
Repeat movements of bars 1 and 2, to end   3–4
in partner's place.
Repeat movements of bars 1 and 2, to end   5–6
in one line as in bars 1 and 2.
Repeat, to end in own places but facing   7–8
partner across the dancing-place.

b BALANCÉ

One Polka step to R.   9
Close feet in 1st position, sway R and L.   10
Repeat these movements to L with l foot.   11–12
Repeat all again to R and L, finishing   13–16
facing forward, each man offering his arm
to his partner.

FIGURE II: CASTING

Odd numbers cast to the L, even numbers   1–16
to the R, to move down the dancing-place
(see Diagram 2); then cast outward and
finish in a double circle facing the centre,
men on the outside behind their partners
(Diagram 3).

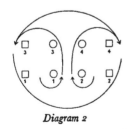

Diagram 2

Diagram 3

LI JARDINIERO

Moderato

Arranged by Arnold Foster

Sian tou - ti gen - to jar - di - nie - ro Que n'a - ven de fru en tout temps, E a - ven li flour li plus bel - lo, Li ven-den tou - ti ben jou - vent._____ Se vou-lis crum-pa de ro - so, De bel-li flour de jaus-se - min,_____ De pes - se - gue_____ de pou-mo ro - so, de pou-mo

33

Women make arches with their hoops by
holding the left side of their own hoop with
their r hand and the right side of their
neighbour's hoop with their l hand.

FIGURE III: ARCHES

The men dance in and out of the arches,
passing in front of the first and behind the
second woman and so on, moving C-C
until back in their own places.

1–16

FIGURE IV: BOWER

No. 1 man takes the left side of his partner's
hoop and moves to the centre of the circle.
The other women follow the first woman
and move C-C round the first man, each in
turn handing him the left side of her hoop,
so that in the end the left side of each hoop
is held by the first man and the other by
each woman (Diagram 4). The other men
remain in their places on the outside.

1–16

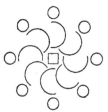

Diagram 4

FIGURE V: ROUND THE BOWER

The women and the first man remain in
this position while the other men move
round the outside C, sometimes facing and
sometimes with their back to the bower.
Each man ends in his own place.

1–16

FIGURE VI
Each woman, starting with the l foot and
moving C-C, takes her hoop from the first
man, and all end in a double circle with
the men on the outside, as in Diagram 3.

1–16

FIGURE VII
Each man now takes the left side of his
partner's hoop in his l hand (she still holds
the right side in her r hand), offers his r
arm to his partner, and all move C to form
a straight line across the dancing-place,
facing forward. In this position they sing
the verse of the song for the second time.

1–16

Sung
verse
second
time

Each man, turning to the L, takes the left
side of his partner's hoop in his r hand.
Each woman holds the right side of her
hoop with the l hand so that a tunnel is
made through which the others all pass.
The first couple now moves forward under
all the arches, followed by the then bottom
couple and all other couples in turn. All
move off.

1–8
or
1–16
as
necessary

A LAUTERBACH

꽃╌꽃╌꽃꽃

Region   Alsace, and in other regions of the Lower and Upper Rhine.

Character   Natural and gay, with simple dramatic expression.

Formation   A dance for any number of couples, partners facing, men hands on hips, women holding their skirts with both hands.

Dance	MUSIC *Bars*
1 16 Swing-hops, beginning on r foot. (Hop on r foot swinging l leg across, slightly diagonally, knee and ankle stretched.)	A 1–16
2 With r hands joined and raised, turn C on the spot with 4 Swing-hops; then turn and join l hands and repeat, turning C-C. Repeat as in bars 17–24.	B 17–24 25–32
3 During this part of the dance there is no singing. Valse with partner round the room with ordinary Valse grasp or with hands on each other's shoulders.	C 33–44

This dance is repeated for each verse of the song, i.e. three times.

A LAUTERBACH

Arranged by Arnold Foster

37

Plate 4   Valse.   Alsace

BIBLIOGRAPHY

PROVENCE

ALFORD, VIOLET.—'The Farandole', with map and tunes. *Journal of the English Folk Dance and Song Society*, December 1932.

—— 'The Baccubert.' *Journal of the E.F.D.S.S.*, December 1940.

—— 'Notes on Three Provençal Dances.' *Journal of the E.F.D.S.S.*, December 1941.

—— 'Dances of Provence.' *The Dancing Times*, March and May 1939.

—— 'The Rigaudon.' *The Musical Quarterly*, New York, July 1944.

—— 'Christmas Carols and Crèches in Provence.' *The Musical Quarterly*, January 1945.

ARAGON, HENRY.—*Les Danses de la Provence et du Roussillon.* 1922.

ARÈNE, PAUL.—*La Chèvre d'Or.* Paris, 1893.

CHARLES-ROUX, JULES.—*Le Costume en Provence.* Paris, 1909.

JUMAND, P., and HÉLÈNE SAUREL.—*Les Bravades.* St-Raphaël, 1927.

MISTRAL, FRÉDÉRIC.—*Calendal.* Avignon, 1867.

—— *Mémoires et récits.* Paris, 1906.

PROVENCE, MARCEL.—*Symbolisme des danses provençales.* Aix-en-Provence, 1937.

—— *Les Chivau Frus.* Aix-en-Provence, 1937.

—— *La Pastorale de Séguret.* Aix-en-Provence, 1935.

VILLENEUVE.—*Statistiques des Bouches-du-Rhône*, vol. III, 1826.

ALSACE

DARGIEUX, ROUART.—*Chansons alsaciennes.* Paris.

KAUFFMANN, P.—*En Alsace ignorée.* Colmar, 1926.

LINCKENHELD, EMILE.—*Quinze ans de folklore alsacien.* Strasbourg.

The following contain dance-songs but no indications of steps or figures:

Les Chants d'Alsace. Musique pour tous, Edition Universelle, Paris.

Chants d'Alsace. Edition Huguenin, Paris.

Chants d'Alsace. La Lyre Chansonnière, Paris.